# Gust
## Three movements from
# The Planets

Mars · Venus · Jupiter
*transcribed for organ*
*by* Arthur Wills

C000133172

# Contents

These arrangements © Copyright 1999 J. Curwen & Sons Ltd.
All rights reserved.
Published in Great Britain by Novello Publishing Limited
Head office: 8/9 Frith Street, London, W1V 5TZ
Tel. 0207-434 0066
Fax 0207-287 6329

Sales and Hire: Music Sales Distribution Centre,
Newmarket Road, Bury St Edmunds, Suffolk IP33 3YB
Tel. 01284 702600  Fax 01284 768301
Web: www.internetmusicshop.com
e-mail: music@musicsales.co.uk

All Rights reserved
Printed in Great Britain
No part of this publication may be copied or reproduced
in any form or by any means without the prior permission
of Novello & Company Limited.

# MARS
## (The Bringer of War)
### (THE PLANETS, I.)

Solo Trumpet 8'*
Gt. Soft Founds. 8'
Sw. Full (box closed)
Ped. 16' 8'
Sw. to Gt.
Gt. & Sw. to Ped.

GUSTAV HOLST
Transcribed by Arthur Wills

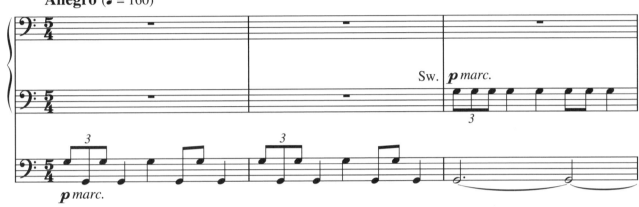

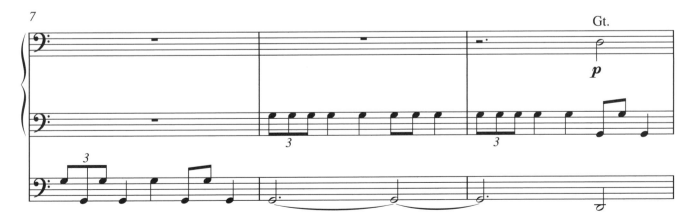

\* Where possible play this from the Choir or Positive manual.

This arrangement © Copyright 1999 J. Curwen & Sons Ltd.

All Rights Reserved

**(poco animato)**

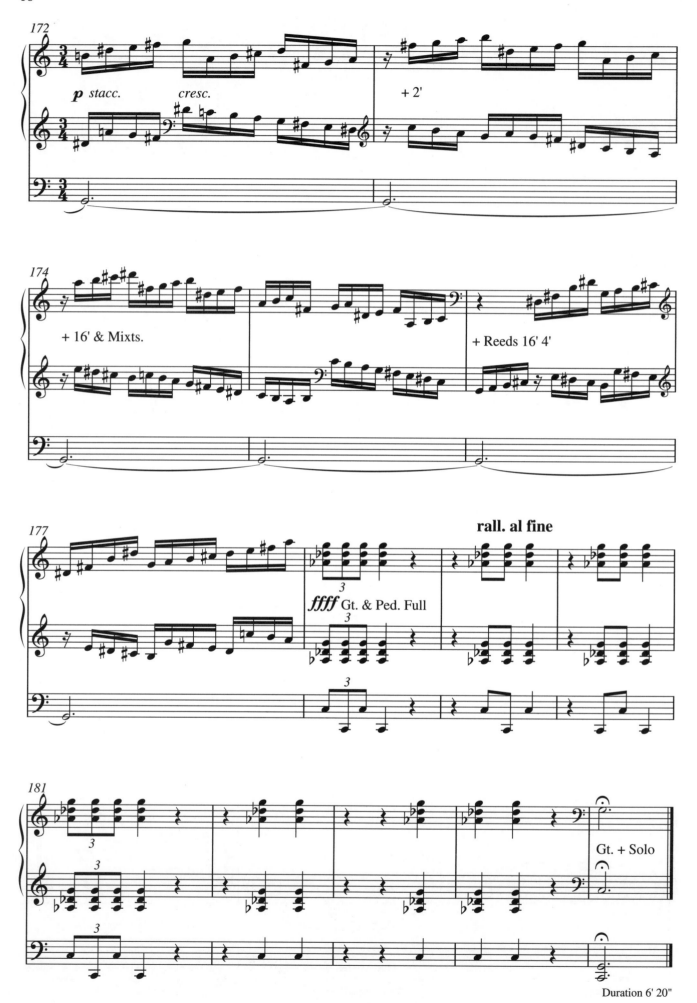

Duration 6' 20"

# VENUS
## (The Bringer of Peace)

### (THE PLANETS, II.)

Sw. Flute 4' (Box open)
Gt. Flute 8'
Ped. Flute 4'
Sw. to Gt.

GUSTAV HOLST
Transcribed by Arthur Wills

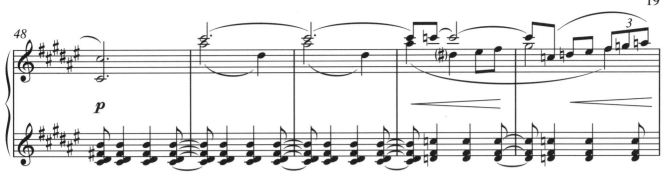

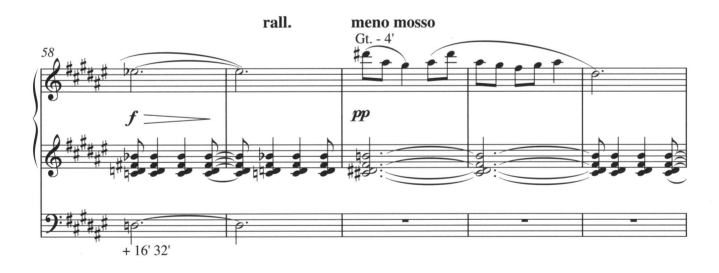
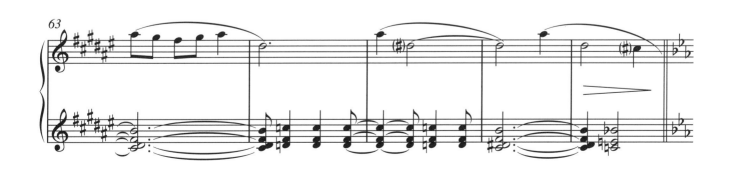

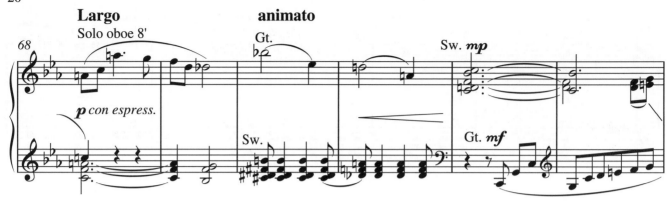

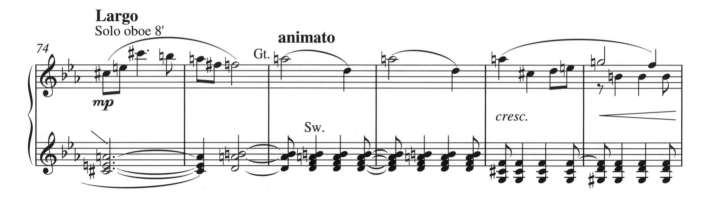

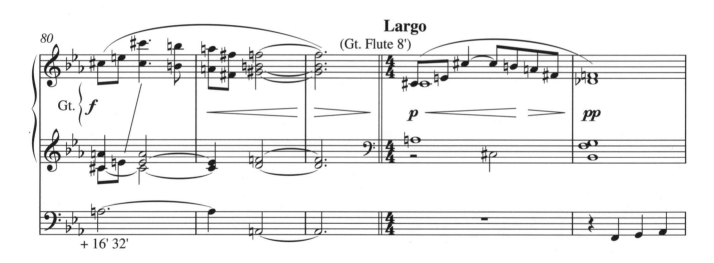

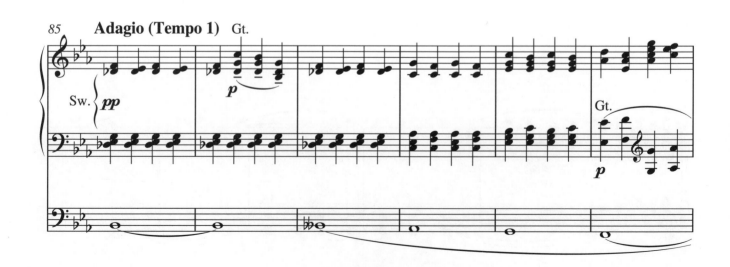

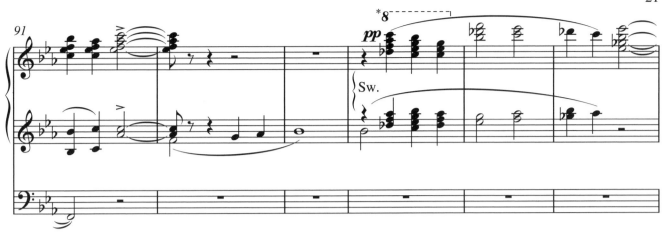

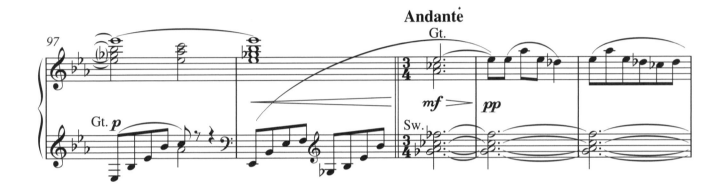

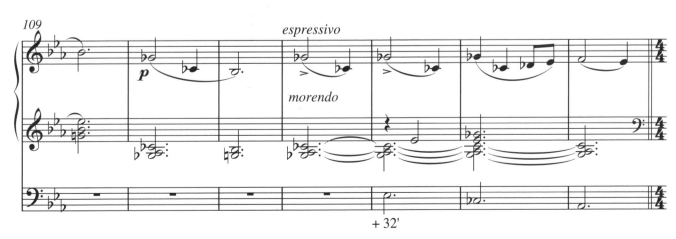

\* If these notes are not available play down an octave +4'.

Duration 6' 20"

# JUPITER
# (The Bringer of Jollity)

### (THE PLANETS, IV.)

Solo Tuba or Trumpet 8' 4'
Gt. Prin. 16' 8' 4' 2'
Sw. Full (Box half open)
Ped. 16' 8' 4'
Sw. to Gt.
Sw. & Gt. to Ped.

GUSTAV HOLST
Transcribed by Arthur Wills

**Allegro giocoso** (♩ = 126)

**= ♪) Tempo 1**

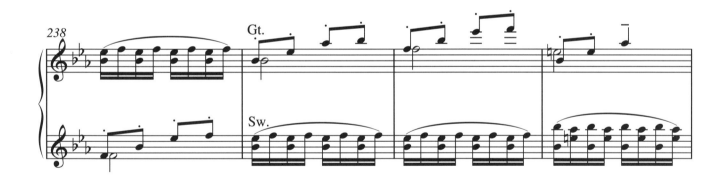

Duration 7' 40"

Printed in the United Kingdom by Caligraving Limited, Thetford, Norfolk.

# 20th century organ music from Novello

| | | |
|---|---|---|
| Jennifer Bate | Four Reflections | NOV 010223 |
| | Homage to 1685 (4 Studies for organ) | NOV 010227 |
| | Introduction and Variations on an Old French Carol | NOV 010176 |
| Richard Rodney Bennett | Alba | NOV 010144 |
| Charles Camilleri | Missa Mundi | NOV 750030 |
| Peter Dickinson | Blue Rose Variations | NOV 010237 |
| | Concerto for Organ | NOV 011000 |
| | Paraphrase 1 | NOV 010129 |
| | Postlude on Adeste Fideles | NOV 590336 |
| | Three Pieces & A Cambridge Postlude | NOV 010173 |
| | Three Statements | NOV 590344 |
| John Gardner | Five Hymn-Tune Preludes | NOV 620010 |
| Peter Hurford | Bristol Suite | NOV 010997 |
| | Two Dialogues | NOV 570032 |
| Francis Jackson | Toccata, Chorale and Fugue | NOV 590275 |
| John Joubert | Passacaglia & Fugue | NOV 620012 |
| | Six Short Preludes on English Hymn Tunes | NOV 360125 |
| Bryan Kelly | Pastorale and Paean | NOV 010998 |
| | Prelude and Fugue | NOV 590327 |
| Nicola LeFanu | Omega | NOV 010204 |
| John McCabe | Dies Resurrectionis | NOV 010213 |
| | Johannis Partita | NOV 620026 |
| | Sinfonia 1961 | NOV 620024 |
| Simon Preston | Vox Dicentis | NOV 010984 |
| Daniel Roth | Joie, Douleur et Gloire de Marie | NOV 010230 |
| Giles Swayne | The Coming of Saskia Hawkins | NOV 360058 |
| | Paraphrase | NOV 360057 |
| | Riff-Raff | NOV 360034 |
| Janet Owen Thomas | Rosaces | NOV 010228 |
| Judith Weir | Ettrick Banks | NOV 360071 |
| | Michael's Strathspey | NOV 360072 |
| | Wild Mossy Mountains | NOV 360075 |
| Malcolm Williamson | Fons Amoris | NOV 620025 |
| | Symphony | NOV 011551 |
| Arthur Wills | Five Pieces | NOV 620013 |
| | Select Organ Works (Eucharistic Suite, Postlude and Prelude and Fugue) | NOV 010210 |
| | Variations on *Amazing Grace* and Toccata | NOV 620030 |
| Hugh Wood | Capriccio Op. 8 | NOV 010135 |

and music by Bliss, Bridge, Elgar, Howells, Leighton, Thalben-Ball, Thiman and others.

*Please request a catalogue*
Novello Publishing Limited
8/9 Frith Street, London, W1V 5TZ
Tel. 0207-434 0066 Fax 0207-287 6329